BEE N'COURAGED

MOMENTS OF MOTIVATION

———————

Sheronda K. Davis

BEE N'COURAGED: MOMENTS OF MOTIVATION
Copyright © 2019 by SHERONDA K. DAVIS

Shannon LeAnn Unlimited, LLC
Publishing Division
P O Box 292017, Columbia, SC 29229
www.pastorshannonmcrae.com

ACKNOWLEDGMENTS

There are so many people to thank. But, first and foremost, I am so grateful to God for never giving up on me, always forgiving me, and sustaining me in my dry places. When I felt I was all alone, God fed me by the brook in the most uncommon ways. Lord, You sustained me so I could get up and keep going, and I'm so grateful. Thank you, Father.

I want to thank my mom because it was in her place that many of these motivational moments happened. When I needed understanding on something you explained it to me. Thanks to my sister for encouraging me and supporting me, love you guys. My son who has grown to be an "N'COURAGER" in his own right. Keep going, you got this!

To my spiritual Mom and Dad, Apostle Allen H. Simmons and Lady Janice Y. Simmons, thank you for always praying for me, and loving and encouraging me.

I want to thank Pastor Shannon for pushing me out the boat and being a mentor to me at the time I needed guidance. You saw it in me and motivated me to move; I love and appreciate you for that, thank you.

I can't name everyone, as that would be a whole other book. Love you all. And as I always say, "Be and let the Bee SPEAK."

It takes courage to grow up and become who you really are. – E.E. Cummings

INTRODUCTION

Moments of Motivation, these "moments" came to me at different times in my life to help inspire and encourage me to see things at a whole other level. MOMENTS OF MOTIVATION is for you to BEE "N'COURAGED" in knowing that, you can see yourself through one of these moments; you can see your issue or an issue you dealt with through one or some of these moments. I've had many moments and at one point I just took it as Him giving me revelation and yes, it is that, but He also gives us moments to encourage us concerning personal matters. My moments are moments, some are "aha" moments.

MOMENTS OF MOTIVATION are just that, moments. Sometimes all it takes is a moment. I loved every moment He has shown me; these moments have helped me to change my perspective on how I was seeing myself and life's situations. These moments of motivation were given to me to reveal things concerning me on beyond what I allowed myself to see regarding my life. I believe I'm a pretty simple person. I love encouraging and inspiring people to see things beyond where they are. These moments of motivation have truly blessed me, and I believe that it will be a blessing to you as well. The thing I love about these moments is the fact that they were shown to me in the simplest of things. Moments of Motivation are like when your body is craving something, but you're not sure what it is, then when that one thing hits your palate, you are in relief like, "Yes, that's what I've been wanting," or "That's what my body needed." Moments of Motivation, I believe, touches on the need. Know that in the writing of this book, these moments are truly from my heart to yours.

We can speak BEE "N'COURAGED" all day, but to those who are struggling or have had troubles and not quite sure what it is to BEE "N'COURAGED," these Moments of Motivation are a step to the process of "N'COURAGEMENT." If you pay close attention, and I'm sure after you read this book you'll have a better understanding, moments of motivation are always trying to be given to you through the course of your day. So, Enjoy these Moments of Motivation. I pray it "N'COURAGES" you to start to see yours.

2 BEE OR NOT 2 BEE

The great poet William Shakespeare asked, "To be, or not to be: that is the question." As in to exist or live? Is it your desire to just exist? Or is there a greater desire to live? Your life has a greater purpose often beyond your imagination. No matter how small or insignificant you may feel, you have a purpose.

I questioned the significance of the bee insect. Bees are some of the hardest working creatures on the planet with a hard work ethic, we owe many thanks to this amazing yet often under-appreciated insect. Ever felt under-appreciated? You work so hard to pursue purpose, yet your contributions go unnoticed. Know that you're not alone.

To be simply means live and exist, occupy a place or position. Similar to the bee insect, small is size, but they have a great impact. They're not bees just to be but bees that produce. Bees are always producing. They aid in keeping and producing outwardly, as well as in the hive. They work as a unified group, and each bee was born with a purpose. That purpose aids in the producing of something of value, honey. Did you

7

know it takes approximately 550 bees to visit approximately two million flower blossoms just to create one pound of honey, not just for their use, but because it's valuable to us? Bees don't know how much of a value it is to us, all they know is to produce.

Bees are some of the hardest working creatures on the planet, and because of their laborious work ethic, we owe many thanks to this amazing yet often under-appreciated insect. Today is the day you start embracing your value, purpose, and strength. BEE "N'COURAGED" today! There is a purpose beyond merely existing. Trust and know what you're going through isn't just for you but it's for someone else. What you're producing is of great value. Bee N'Couraged this day and keep producing.

NO LONGER A DEFAULT

Years ago, I had a bad habit; I smoked for approximately 10 years. It was a daily routine. Morning, noon, and night and in between I had to attend to my nicotine addiction. I'd even awaken in the middle of the night for a few pulls and go back to sleep. Indeed, it was a bad habit. For years it was embedded in my DNA, or at least that's what I figured. I would often try to convince myself to stop but the struggle was real. It was my norm, but that would soon end. I had to make a conscious decision to regain control of my life and health, but my cigarette habit was completely consuming me. I began the process of smoking cessation by regaining mind control. I had to resist the urge to smoke until the desire decreased

A habit is a settled or regular tendency or practice, especially one that is hard to give up. I've been told that it takes 21 days to break a habit. That seemed unrealistic to me, I figured it depended on the habit. We take ownership of our habits, therefore, they become difficult to break. This can be quite discouraging when you have an inner desire to quit, but the reality is your life appears to be in desperate need of it. Likewise, discouragement is like a bad habit, once you get used to it, you depend on it, you look for it, and take ownership of it. Discouragement is a loss of confidence or enthusiasm and many times through lies, trials, disappointments, and rejection we make it a habit to remain in that condition. We spend a lot of time telling others to Bee "N'Couraged" because we know what the opposite feels like.

Today I declare being discouraged is no longer a default. Break the cycle, break the habit! Whether it's negative thoughts, failed expectations, or even your failure to expect more, you have the power to create a new norm. Focus on positive behaviors and regain mind control. Consider positive affirmation and read the Word of God daily. Faith comes by hearing and hearing by the Word of God. Make reading the Word your default, your automatic go to. Don't go back to your old way of thinking. You don't live there any longer. Remain confident and stop falling back into old patterns. Grab a journal and write down your thoughts. Then submit those thoughts to God. He is there to keep you from going back to the place you once were.

SPEAK PEACE

If you have children or have experienced being around children for any length of time, you know that they are busybodies. They don't realize it, for they're only children wanting to play and have fun. The busyness and noise can be a bit overwhelming and can be very distracting. Sometimes you've got to take a moment and speak peace. You just got to take a moment, breathe, and step outside of the commotion. Often the first thing that comes to mind is to yell their name and tell them to stop or sit down and be quiet. This is generally how we manage when things get out of hand.

As you go through your day intentionally being "N'COURAGED", understand that distraction, noise, and commotion can throw you off. But you have the power to manage the situation. The atmosphere is calling for peace. I've gone through situations in which everything was coming at me all at once, I knew I needed peace. I was reminded of how Jesus spoke to the storm in Mark 4:39 and commanded peace.

Jesus stood strong and said, "Peace, be still." Then, the wind ceased, and there was a great calm. He called peace into a situation that seemed out of control, then He spoke instructions, "Be still" to the wind. Realize that you have control over what is going on around you, you must get to a place of taking a stand.

KEEP GROWING

One day as I was coming in from work something caught my attention as I pulled into my mom's yard. The grass caught my full attention. She had told me not too long before that she had it cut, but I never really paid too much attention to it until that day. As I am pulling up, I said to myself "Lord, that grass grew fast." While parking and focusing on the grass, I considered the grass does what it is purposed to do, grow. No matter how many times it's walked on or cut down, it grows back. No matter what you're going through go through and grow. Don't' allow what you're going through make you question your purpose.

So, let me ask you, "Does what seem to be coming up against you make you question yourself? Do you sometimes feel like you are strong in you knowing your purpose but then something or someone does or says something that puts you in a place of saying, "Well, maybe this is not what I should be doing" Let me "N'COURAGE" you; like the grass, you add beauty to the atmosphere in being you and doing what it is you're purposed to do. Because if He can let us know that He even shows and sees the purpose in the grass, He sees the same and greater for you. You have a purpose today to reflect on the fact that no matter what seems to be coming up around you BEE "N'COURAGED" to stand strong in knowing you are purposed to do what you do. And if you're not sure of that purpose, let today be the day you reflect on what that may be.

It takes the rain and the sun to aid in growth. So, BEE "N'COURAGED" and stand strong knowing and being able to walk in your purpose and growing in your purpose; there will be some good days and some rainy days but know it all aids in your growth. Remember that all things work together for the good of them who love the Lord (Romans 8:28).

WATCH THOSE DEER

In my opinion, deer are some of the cutest animals. They seem so harmless. It's just something about those eyes, the innocence. They just look like they cannot harm. One day I was at my mom's house, you know that country living. So, I decided to step outside on her back porch only to see her standing out in the field, looking at the spot where she and some neighbors had planted their harvest. She was standing akimbo with this look on her face like she was thinking hard. I knew something was wrong. So, I asked her what the issue was. She answered that the deer were getting into the field and eating the vegetation. She soon began working on some strategies.

She attempted a few things to keep those deer from coming to eat and destroy what she and others had worked so hard to plant. First, she closed the gate, but that didn't stop them from getting into the field and eating the vegetation because, one, there were other open points for them to get in, and two, deer are good jumpers. Now what she did next may seem strange to you because I know it was a little strange to me. But she gathered some tin pie pans and some string while I wondered about what she planned to do with them. Next, she connected them, set them on stacks, and strategically placed them throughout the field. When I saw her doing this, I asked her what she was doing. She said to me, "When the deer come into the field and rub against the string or when the wind blows, it can cause noise and spook them." At that time, I didn't realize deer were easily spooked.

I have learned and still learning through this Moment of Motivation and I want to "N'COURAGE" you today to always be in a place of watching and praying because the enemy of your harvest doesn't have a certain look. And it doesn't matter if what they say or do looks harmless to you, but the more you leave it unattended, the more it is destroying not just your harvest, but also other people who will benefit from what you took time to grow.

SO, BEE "N'COURAGED" to be strategic and know how to keep the enemy at bay. BEE "N'COURAGED" to know that your harvest is of value and there is a sound that fights for you. Surround your harvest with words of encouragement, with prayer, and uplifting praise.

YOU GOT THIS

Have you ever been in a place, like a new job or just doing something new and different in your life? I've experienced a couple of job transitions and I've been on jobs for lengthy time frames. But when I began those jobs in the beginning, I would look at them and feel opposed to them because nothing was familiar to me. I'd watch people do it with ease and say, "Oh my gosh, that is a lot to know, that's a lot of responsibility," and I wasn't sure about doing the job.

I recall one job in particular that I was given. As they took me to the area where the job was, and I watched those machine operators run that machine, I wondered why in the world they chose me for such a job. I was fine and comfortable with where I was at the time. But it seemed that the ones offering me the job believed in me more than I wanted to believe in myself. When I asked the young man why I was selected for the job, his response was "because we believe you can do the job."

On any new job position, there has to be some training for that position. But because it was new to me, it looked to be too much and too difficult. I kept telling myself I couldn't do it. Anything we continually speak to ourselves, we begin to believe. But as time went on, I kept picking it up, getting the information that was given to me, and getting the work done. I was no longer feeding my thoughts with what I couldn't do, but I was applying the skills I learned in training to do my new job effectively. And so, it was when I moved and had to begin again on another job.

Anything that we may do at first may seem difficult and sometimes we just want to put it down and think ourselves into believing we can't do it. I just want to "N'COURAGE" you today, You Got This. Don't allow negative thoughts to fill your mind about what you are purposed to do. Know that before you were even formed in the womb, you had a purpose. And anything you are set to do, know that just like the last thing you conquered, you will conquer this. Be easy on yourself.

There is an area of trial and error, and it's okay. Keep going. I just know and believe that if God allows in His perfect will for you to be there, He will keep you. Isn't it just encouraging to know that God Himself has that much confidence in your ability? He sees what you don't see in yourself. BEE "N'COURAGED" to go through this day with a positive MOTIVATED mind of victories. With God, there is a history of victories.

YOU GOT THIS.

CALL IT FORTH

Today, we call it forth. You never know the thoughts of people. They may be smiling outwardly and battling on the inside. Today, we are speaking in power. And as you read this, say your name, and believe for your manifestation.

Lift your heads oh ye gates and be lifted up ye everlasting doors and the king of glory shall come in (Psalm 24:7).

I am so "N'Couraged" right now, even though some things don't seem to turn out the way I like or think they should, I remain "N'Couraged" because I believe that all things work together for my good. Even when people aren't who I thought they were, I remain "N'Couraged," because I know he told me he'd never leave me nor forsake me. I remain "N'Couraged" even as life throws some hard blows knowing I got this because I am more than a conqueror. I remain "N'Couraged." And, even so, this is a place I've never been in while, yes, at the same time feeling, seeing familiar situations and circumstances, but you know what... I remain

"N'Couraged" because my faith level shows me I am not who I used to be. I am more, yes, I am "N'Couraged" even in my struggle to bee "N'Couraged." Yes, I am. I remain "N'Couraged" and staying focused on and in the one who I know has me. God is faithful, he is the substance. I hope in him, I believe in him, I trust in him. So, my faith says today, because of the greater that's in me, I am more than a conqueror. My faith says I am victorious.

What is your faith saying today? You call it forth. The great I am is faithful. Bee "N'Couraged" today.

RECONSTRUCTION

Reconstruction is a thing that has been rebuilt after being damaged or destroyed; to establish or assemble again. Have you ever walked past a home or building that looked rundown with broken windows that don't look fit for anything, only to see a "FOR SALE" sign posted? Immediately we see this, we think, "Who in the world would want to buy this place? It's not good for anything. Who in the world would want to waste their time and money on this? How about if you were a buyer and you saw this building?" And in most cases, many people would pass by it and think it's not worth the effort, not worthy at all, ugly to look at, can't do anything with it, or needs to be torn down. I know because I've done it.

There was this one house that every time I visited my mom, I would look at it and wonder why it was still standing. To me, it looked like it needed to be torn down. But every time I rode down that street, there it stood. Then I started noticing cars pulling up to this place and I wondered why. Now even though we see no value in this place, someone else comes to buy it because of the potential they see in it. So, the right opportunity is given to begin the work. So, first, by taking ownership of the property, he can evaluate what he has invested in. It's good to check the heart of the house, the foundation. Check the grounds to see if the soil is rich enough for planting, or if something needs to be uprooted. There is so much work to do, but we believe it's worth the effort. Looking at what's inside, everything there must be thrown away because you can't use this old rundown stuff in the new home. Next the attention shifts to the walls. Are they sturdy? What do they look like? What's hiding in the walls? Are they infested? If they are, we tear them down and build a new one because we don't want it to go back to being infested. We replace the windows and doors and check the framework holding them so that, irrespective of the season, it will be able to maintain and sustain leaks, cracks, or worn-down seals. Ok so now it's coming together. Some minor glitches but nothing that can't be handled. Every old thing is replaced with new things. When finished, it looks and smells new, since all things are new. I knew it could be done, reconstructing a building to make it livable.

This motivational moment was when I realized what was done for me.

BEE "N'COURAGED" to know that He loves you just this much. That's what He has done for you, He took the old you- the you that looked rundown, beat-up, and had shattered areas of your life; the you that many, including yourself, may have looked on and treated as worthless, and transformed you.

22

Understand you were bought with a price. He brought you out and every area of reconstruction has to do with what Jesus did just for you. He tore down walls and rebuilt them for you to be strengthened in Him. Understand that the open areas, the areas that leaked were wrong thoughts, wrongly spoken words, and unnecessary THINGS that entered and caused an infestation.

BEE "N'COURAGED" to be grateful for the reconstruction. What others saw as worthless God made it, so He could say IT IS GOOD...

1 Peter 2:5 (ESV)

You yourselves like living stones are being built up as a spiritual house, to be a holy priesthood, to offer spiritual sacrifices acceptable to God through Jesus Christ.

DELAYED BUT NOT DENIED

Let me ask. Have you ever been in a place where you thought you got up early enough to get moving and take care of everything you need to do, especially knowing you were on a tight schedule? Especially when there is somewhere you need to be like work or an appointment. And as you go through the day doing what you're doing, you get delayed repeatedly. For instance, traffic could be extra heavy, there was an accident, or you didn't catch the train. It just seems like whatever could delay you from getting to where you need to be on time is happening. With all the delays, you just know you are going to be late getting to where you needed to be. All you can think at this point is how late you are going to be. You get a little frustrated, maybe not even a little a lot, and to your amazement, with all the delays, you still made it on time.

I've had a similar experience that happened to me. I had a speaking engagement and left in enough time, or so I thought. There were a few things I needed to do before I got to my destination. As I settled in for the drive, suddenly, I noticed the traffic slowing down, and before I knew it, everything came to a complete stop. I mean there was no moving traffic on the interstate and I had to go by my mom's to get a few things done and to pick her up. Let me tell you she lives like 30 minutes away from the church. Finally, after a complete traffic standstill for over an hour and a half, traffic began moving and I still had to drive for about a good hour to get to my mom's. So, you know currently, I was trying to figure it out in my head.

I reached out and called to let it be known I was running behind schedule, and with calmness, they said I should be safe. I got to my mom's house and I felt like I was on warp speed trying to get things done and leave. When I looked at my watch and noticed it was already close to the time I needed to be there, I felt some kind of way about that. Things just kept playing in my head to not even try to go because "you're already late and you're going to miss it." But I kept going thinking, "Well, if I'm not able to do it this time, I can only hope I'm given another opportunity to speak." Everything I felt could go wrong went wrong. I called my Associate Pastor with every step and he kept encouraging me. While on the road, he said, "Okay, be safe" and instructed me on what to do. So, I made it there and even though it wasn't at the time I wanted to be there, I still made it and was able to deliver the message. This experience MOTIVATED me to know and understand that it's in the timing of God. However, we always hope that things happen one way, at a certain time, and in a certain way.

26

I want to "N'COURAGE" you today to not be so hard on yourself because there is an appointed time. To you, it may seem too late, but keep pursuing your purpose. What you have is needed and it will happen on time because someone needs what you have. Yes, the delays will come, but stay focused and keep going. Though it tarries, wait on it, for it will not tarry forever. Delayed, but not denied. You got this.

2 Peter 3:9 (AMP)

"The Lord does not delay and is not tardy or slow about what He promises, according to some people's conception of slowness, but He is long-suffering (extraordinarily patient) toward you, not desiring that any should perish, but that all should turn to repentance."

DON'T BE ANXIOUS

Okay, how many have had this happen to you? You're in a store and you see a piece of cake or something that looks so good and you stop and eye it for a nice minute, saying that looks so good because they have it set up so nice that it grabs your whole attention. You decide to pick it up and take it home. When you get home, you get comfortable and grab that cake or whatever it may have been and get the best thing that compliments it: milk, coffee, ice cream (whatever your preference). You grab your fork, spoon, etc. and position it just right to slice into it. You bring it to your mouth (that may be watering at this point). It smells so good and, in the mouth, it goes and... What just happened here? You waited and wanted that thing so much to only find out it's not what it seemed. Wow, how do we allow what we see to be about what we want? How dangerous is that?

I've learned through many experiences like this (no, not always food) that the thing that you may always seem to want so bad according to what you see is not always what's best for you. Some things come to grab our focus because of the way they are set up and/or the way they may look. When they take our focus, they make us ignore what we are purposed to do. So, through experience, we deal with wanting that man or that woman, or whatever your cake may be that once you get, it wasn't all it appeared to be. It left a nasty taste not just in your mouth.

I've learned that everything that may look good and may come with what seems to be the right ingredient doesn't always mean that it was put together to be good. Your worth says you don't have to settle for anything that leaves a bad taste in your spirit.

THE SOUND

I was reminded of a time in my life (which wasn't that long ago) that I believed that I had no opinion or a voice to speak on certain things. I didn't even like the sound of my voice, so I truly tried not to speak. It was quite embarrassing and very frightening for me. As the years went on, it got a little better, but I still struggled with being in front of people. My thought was, "What do I have to say that people would want to hear?" To me, there were so many other people out there that could and were doing it, so why me?

This motivation moment came back to me from years ago when I was in the choir. We would be singing, and as long as my voice was drowning in with others, it was okay. Then we had this one song where the choir director had us hold a note for what seemed a long period of time, everyone was so winded. And as we all held the note, we all were stopping and taking breaths and it just sounded a mess, it sounded like we were struggling to hold that note. Then he stopped and explained to us what is known as stagger breathing. Now I'm no singer, but for those of you who are, you probably know and get exactly what it is and can relate to this moment. Stagger breathing is when each person takes a breath at different times during a song. That way it didn't break the sound.

Pursue your purpose with confidence. Yes, someone may be doing what you do, but that's their sound. Your voice in the earth and your purpose is very important. I had a chorus director that knew when I was singing or just moving my mouth. He knew when I needed to sing up because he couldn't hear me, I wondered how that was. But when you are equipped and trained to hear every note from every individual, it becomes easy. The one who called you to your purpose knows your voice and has confidence in your sound. So yes, there will be times you feel winded and in need of a breath, know that while you get your second wind, you're covered by the continuous flow of sound in the atmosphere. I just want to "N'COURAGE" you today to know that your voice counts. Your voice and your purpose are for those that will know your sound regardless of how many are doing what you do. So instead of asking, "Why me?" the question should be, "Why not me?" Whatever it is you are called to do in the earth, it has a sound. Even though it may get tiring, BEE "N'COURAGED" to know that people are holding their sound while you catch your breath to carry on.

DECISIONS, DECISIONS

One thing I had to realize and I notice about me is that I would let my feelings dictate my decisions. Whatever was in my thought process that's what I would go with concerning me, how I saw me and my situations. I allowed what other's thought of me dictate my decisions.

I visited my aunt in the hospital some time ago. My cousin and I sat talking about the goodness of God and began discussing car trouble. She was having some issues with it and was trying to get some assistance in fixing it. She proceeded to say the technician kept trying to force the diagnostic work that needed to be done. She, however, didn't allow his pushy ways to dictate her decision. She decided to ask for a supervisor. Her stance was this, "I don't argue with people who don't make decisions."

This was a motivational moment, My God Yes! Let me encourage someone right now. There is always a struggle with our emotions and thoughts, it's a daily battle. But the question I have for you today is,

WHOSE REPORT WILL YOU BELIEVE? During every difficult battle, struggle, or situation you must know the Author and Finisher of Our Faith. Include Him in your plans. Move forward in the things of God and stand on His final Word. People will laugh, talk, and scorn you because of your plans and decisions, but God has a plan for your life. Don't retaliate, stand still and know, DON'T ARGUE WITH PEOPLE WHO DON'T MAKE DECISIONS concerning you because quiet as kept, God will decide between them as well.

IT'S JUST A HURDLE

Every time we have purposed in our hearts to do right or get back in line, there seems to always be something that comes along and throws a stumbling block in the way. Most of the time we let it get the best of us. A hurdle is one of a series of upright frames over which athletes in a race must jump. A hurdle is also defined as an obstacle or difficulty. Today's action plan: Keep Pressing.

Just as in a race, hurdles may be set up back to back, but you master them and keep going. Just as you leap over one, there will be another. I'm no track expert but I am N'Couraged to Keep Going!

A track runner prepares for the hurdles ahead. With time, practice, and patience they learn through a process of repetition and timing. They follow the instructions of the trainer and prepare to be physically and psychologically able to master the hurdles. The finish line is the goal, they just have to skillfully cross over each hurdle.

Don't be thrown off by the hurdles in life. Stay focused on the goal. Follow the instructions of the Head Coach and you'll make it. Every once and a while you will stumble over a hurdle, but you can get up and keep going. The hurdles are building and strengthening you to endure. Recover quickly! Romans 8:37 "Nay, in all these things we are more than conquerors through him that loved us."

5S - TIGHTEN UP

The philosophy of 5S represents a way of focusing and thinking to better organize and manage a workspace, specifically by eliminating the 8 Wastes as defined by the Lean Manufacturing system. The 5s consists of sort, set in order, shine, standardize (stabilize), and sustain (self-discipline). This is used to help establish order. And to keep us updated, we are required to attend 5s training. In training, the instructor went through each of the steps in THE 5s.

To sort means to go through what you have and discard what you're not going to keep or what you're not using. This step focuses on the elimination of any unnecessary workplace clutter. SORT asks questions like,

- "What's the purpose of this?"

- " When was it last used?"

- "How often and is it needed?"

Sorting's benefits include more effective use of space, simplified tasks, a reduction in hazards, and a significant decrease in distracting clutter.

Set in Order – The goal of this step is to examine methods of storage that are effective and efficient, sometimes referred to as "visual management," and then create a work environment that is organized, ergonomic, uncluttered and easily navigable. Some questions to ask during this step might be: Which specific items are needed to perform a task? How many items need to be readily accessible and where should they be located?

Shine – With the clutter gone and the storage organized, the next step is to properly and thoroughly clean the work area every day. This step is critical as a way of sustaining the improvements begun in the Sort and Set phases. All storage areas, machines, equipment, tools, and work surfaces must be cleaned and checked regularly. Employees will feel more comfortable in this clean and uncluttered environment, which could also lead to increased ownership of the organization's goals and vision.

Standardize – Now that the first three steps are in play, it's time to standardize these new practices. All employees need to be included in the creation of a set of standards that will become the new norm for the workspace. When these new standards and best practices are implemented, the old habits will soon die out and be replaced by the more efficient patterns of behavior. New standards, however, will probably require some oversight and enforcement until they are habitual; reminders such as visuals and emails are effective tools to help these new standards become set in stone.

Sustain – The final step of 5S is certainly the most challenging: remaining disciplined enough to sustain the positive changes made in the first three steps. It is critical that the new system be maintained or the efforts and costs put into developing the new system will be pointless. By putting a formal system in place that includes regular training and communication, employees will be able to comfortably conform to the company's 5S procedures.

The 5S system is not complicated to understand; the challenges lie in successfully implementing the steps and sustaining the practices. Among other things, a successful 5S implementation will improve workplace safety, develop self-esteem among employees and reduce training time for new employees.

Systems must be in place to effectively carry out the thing you're trying to accomplish. It isn't a foolproof system but rather a system of procedures to maximize and improve workplace safety and increase productivity.

God's Word sets a standard in our lives. You must ask yourself sometimes the hard questions you may not want the answer to. Ask yourself, "Is this (friendship/relationship) worth holding on to?" Is what has been set in order sustainable? Hold on to everything good to set it in order. Every day, shine up your new way by staying in prayer, reading your word, and keeping the right mindset. Sustaining this will take self-discipline to keep it going; it's an ongoing process every day.

God uses what we go through to tighten us up. Are you getting the lesson? Life's happenings come to grow us and cause us to set things in order. God is a God of order. He always sees the best in you. Respond quickly to the Word of God and watch your inclination to pull away from what God is doing. Trust in the Lord continually because He is doing great work in you. Be done with old habits and develop a new standard of behavior. It takes a lot to Bee N'Couraged but you've got what it takes.

THE TILLING

Till is defined as to labor, as by plowing or harrowing, upon (land) for the raising of crops; cultivate; to plow. It also means to cultivate the soil. One morning at my mom's house, I awakened to the sound of what I believed was a tractor plowing my mom's field. As I lay there listening to the sound of the tractor, what I came to understand through a Moment of Motivation was that we underestimate the equipment that is used to turn the soil and the process of tilling the ground in preparation of a new harvest. Without the process, the ground would never be ready to yield a harvest.

My mom shared with me one day as I sat and watched a neighbor come with his tractor to prepare the ground for planting the seed. She said that there is a process of preparing for the next harvest. The soil must be turned up to remove the roots from the old harvest. He came and did that a few times, I was told the old has to dry up to plant the new or the roots from the previous harvest will grow with the new and could choke out the new harvest.

So understand that in all things, give thanks, for this is the will of God concerning you. Let the tilling do what it does, we need it for our harvest. Don't allow your past to hinder or choke out what you are purposed to do. Remain Kingdom minded. The Keeper of the ground and what He uses to bring about growth and harvest knows exactly what He is doing. Romans 12:2 says, "Do not be conformed to this world, but be transformed by the renewal of your mind." When you renew your mind through Scripture, you allow the Bible to transform your heart into fertile soil that bears everlasting fruit.

SHIFTING THE ATMOSPHERE

While I was about to get off from work, the lighting in the plant started getting a little dim. So, I looked around and said to the lady next to me, "You know it looked like this yesterday just before it started to rain. You know the atmosphere on the outside affects the inside?" I immediately caught that in my spirit. Looking at her excited, I said, "THAT'S A WORD!!! I RECEIVE IT! THANK YOU!"

I got excited from the simple fact of knowing from my own experiences that when things would happen in my life, I would take on a different attitude immediately and that attitude would go along with the situation. Like if my bills were behind, I would be worried and concerned, trying to think of what I could do knowing I didn't have the money. Did that change my situation? No, because the bill was still due.

WHEN YOUR MOOD ON THE INSIDE STARTS TO FEEL DARK AND DIM, CHECK YOUR OUTSIDE ATMOSPHERE!!! WHAT'S TRYING TO CLOUD YOUR FOCUS? WHAT'S

CLOUDING YOUR SUN?!!! Yes, the storms (issues) come, but we have the breath of God in us. Speak to the cloud (issue), move the cloud from blocking your source of life, of growth, and of health. 1 John 4:4 (NIV) You, dear children, are from God and have overcome them, because the one who is in you is greater than the one who is in the world.

You have the power and authority to speak and decree a thing and it is established (Romans 4:17). Use your mouth and shift the atmosphere!

WEATHERMAN

Every region has its favorite weatherman. And for some of us, it's someone in our family (my mom). During certain times of the year, she advises we watch the weather closely. Living in the Lowcountry (Charleston, SC) hurricane season is a huge deal. Storms seem to appear out of nowhere. One of the main things my mom asks is "what does the weather look like"? The main duties of meteorologists include recording and analyzing data from worldwide weather stations, satellites, radars, and remote sensors. interpreting observations from the land, sea and upper atmosphere. They use the information collected to track and keep an eye on what's going on with the weather, and they will inform us of predicted outcomes. They track thunderstorms and tropical storms that may be developing on the water. So, it's rare when we get bad weather or storms that we had not already anticipated or heard of to help us prepare mentally and get the supplies needed to weather whatever storm that comes.

My mom would always practice emergency preparedness; she would periodically buy candles, batteries, and certain non-perishable foods in preparation for what could happen in the future. We seemed to have these things in excess and could not figure out why because we'd hardly use any of the items unless we encountered a storm. The storms that come in your life are being tracked by our Head Weather Man. Don't be caught off guard by your storm. Stay connected and pay attention to the chief meteorologist (Jesus). He teaches us through the Holy Spirit how to prepare for the storms of life through fasting, prayer, and meditation of His Word.

Don't think about the bad weather, but instead seek peace through Christ. Meditate on His promises and be strong. The sun doesn't always have to be out to give the Lord thanks so continue to give Him praise.

Psalm 107:28-31 Yet when they cried out to the Lord in their trouble, the Lord brought them out of their distress. He calmed the storm and its waves quieted down. So they rejoiced that the waves became quiet, and he led them to their desired haven. Let them give thanks to the Lord for his gracious love and his awesome deeds on behalf of mankind.

NOT DISCREDITED

I love God, He is always there loving on us, even when He is correcting us. God, I thank you this day for encouraging and strengthening me. Today, I thank Him for just a little taste of showing me I AM NOT discredited (having lost one's reputation).

I was talking to my mom today about my nephew who joined the Navy. I said to her, "Just because you're in the military doesn't mean you make a lot of money at the start, but you have access to a lot of stuff." When I got that download, I began to bless the Lord. I could only thank Him because my faith in Him increased at that moment. The FAVOR of God gives you access to stuff you or others thought you could never have. And it's so much greater than our thought process.

It's not about what you start with. Bee N'Couraged by the Favor of God on your life. People will often discredit you based on your current location in life. Having less doesn't mean you've lost. When God strips you of certain things doesn't mean you lost.

1 Samuel 30:8 and David inquired of the LORD, "Shall I pursue this raiding party? Will I overtake them?" "Pursue them," he answered. "You will certainly overtake them and succeed in the rescue." The people in David's town tried to discredit him based on his current situation, but he encouraged himself in the Lord. His faith gave him access to victory!

POWER WALK

On a previous job, a few of my coworkers and I would get together on our 10-minute break and start walking laps. On one occasion, I was left to walk alone (I didn't like that). I started to change my mind because I just didn't want to do it alone. I pushed the idea aside and went on with it. I pressed in spite of how I felt. As I walked, my focus changed. As I started walking, the lights caught my attention. Now, on this job, they had these motion sensor lights, where if there's no movement, the lights shut themselves down, but as soon as it senses motion the lights immediately came on. Initially, I paid no attention to it, but the more I moved, I noticed a change. I then began taking intentional steps forward to provoke the lighting, I'm walking with my head up, taking more powerful strides, enjoying watching the lights as I catch a Moment of Motivation.

This walk showed me that this is who I am, a power walker. Joshua 1:3 I will give you every place you set your feet as I promised Moses. Understand that it's okay if, sometimes, you have to take that walk by

49

yourself just, so God can show you who you are through His Word. To give you a power walk in confidence.

I want to "N'COURAGE" you as it "N'COURAGED" me, this is how you walk. This is what's in you – Light. We are called to be a light. Every time you put your foot down, there should be light. Your faith gives you a power walk that will allow you and others to see results regardless of "your issues". So, head up, chest out, powerful strides.

GRATEFUL

1 Thessalonians 5:18 (NLT) Be thankful in all circumstances, for this is God's will for you who belong to Christ Jesus. Be excited about what God is doing in your life. Try your best not to focus so much on your past. Your past is just that, gone by in time and no longer existing, It no longer has the power or authority to hold on you any longer. Believe what God has said concerning you. There will be difficult times in your life but be grateful even in the midst of it. Do your best not to put your hands in what He's preparing. God's delay is not a denial, remain thankful that some things He didn't allow because of the damage it could've caused. God is Sovereign, He does what He wants to do when He wants to. It will not always feel good to our flesh, but He knows what's best.

Remember the enemy is a deceiver, think about it. At the time your spirit was growing, along came something or someone who caused you to slowly, and without awareness, drift right back into what you knew and no longer desired. It's like a regifted gift, the same thing but with different wrapping.

God is faithful. Stand strong in freedom, be grateful for what He didn't allow. Whatever the outcome, remain grateful. He always has a way of encouraging you to know you are more. You are right where you need to be. Everything you went through {discouragement, deceit, unfruitful relationships} is going to work for your good. Rejoice in the fact you endured and came out with the victory. It proves that God is for you. Nothing that anyone has done against you will prosper. Love people beyond what they've done to you.

Accept what God allows. Follow His lead. If He is saying let it go, let it go. Don't fight against His Will. Things come in our lives whether good or bad to help us grow. Keep going and keep growing!

THE FALL

The legendary Gospel Songwriter, Tramaine Hawkins,
penned these words,
I've lost some good friends along life's way
Some loved ones departed in heaven to stay
But thank God I didn't lose everything
I've lost faith in people who said they cared
In time of my crisis they were never there
But in my disappointment, in my season of pain
One thing never wavered, one thing never changed
I never lost my hope,
I never lost my joy
I never lost my faith
But most of all, I never lost my praise.

I remembered singing along with this song and had to
stop myself because for me that just wasn't true...I
had lost all that. The thing about it is, I wasn't sure if I
could get it back or if I even wanted it back because
of my fall. Yes, my fall, my spiritual fall. What seemed
to be the most devasting and embarrassing moment
of my life turned out later to be a Moment of

Motivation. I was at work trying to get myself together, so I could end my shift. I knew I had reported on how the line ran. I was so preoccupied with trying to remember everything while at the same time switching my attention to the person I needed to talk to. Since I was in a hurry, I made my way in her direction and did not realize what I was in for. As I walked toward her with my things in my hand, I took my focus off where I was walking and all I felt was my legs hit something. I thought I caught my balance, but I was wrong, down I went along with everything in my hands and I hit the floor. I heard people calling me and I wasn't that badly hurt, but I experienced some pain. All I could do was lie there and not move. Initially, because I was in shock followed by shame. I knew I needed to get up, but I couldn't, and I wasn't sure if I even wanted to get up. I felt one person on each side of me grab my arms and helped me up and walked with me to get assistance at the nurse's station. I remember hearing people laugh. My greatest pain was within. My supervisor came to see if I was okay. I asked if I had to come in tomorrow and he said: "yes because you're not that bad off." But my pride was hurt pretty badly.

I showed up in physical pain. People still laughed and looked, but I was determined to work. I kept showing up day after day, the pain subsided as well as the embarrassment. My spiritual fall had me just like this natural fall. When I told my mom about it, she said: "well, at least, you got up."

Let me "N'COURAGE" you today that yes, it's a hard place. What this taught me was to stay focused. Watch the distraction and always be mindful of what the enemy can and will use to keep you from your purpose. Yes, it happened and caused pain but know people are holding you up and willing to walk with you in the place of your pain to get to your HEALING and to the One who knows. Forgive yourself and keep moving because as you continue in purpose, the pain that was at one point so great will be a memory and a testimony of your getting up.

Psalm 37:23-24 The LORD directs the steps of the godly. He delights in every detail of their lives. Though they stumble, they will never fall, for the LORD holds them by the hand.

IT'S A DOOR

I'm reminded of a time when I was entering my mom's yard, and out of all the times I had been in and out of her yard, I never took notice to her door. I mean it never really caught my attention. I remember saying, as I drove in the yard looking at her front door, that the paint was wearing off, the paint was all chipped up and falling off. It didn't look appealing at all. I looked at it saying, "Lord, look at that door, it doesn't look right, it's an eyesore." Then the question came back to me, "Does it make the door any less of a door? Does it still function as a door even with its broken, chipped-off pieces?"

I want to "N'COURAGE" you today with this motivational moment that yes, you may have experienced sometimes of brokenness. I know the feeling all too well, some chipped-off pieces. It was necessary for the restoration process. People, places, and things over time chip away, but again it was necessary. Know that it doesn't make you any less of who you are. You begin to acknowledge your worth in the process. It's during this time you start to see who God has made and called you to be. A door is a door and it has a purpose. Although tarnishing happens over time and bolts may loosen, the door does its job. Know this and stand sure in this that you can do all things through Christ Who strengthens you (Phil 3:14). Find strength in your ability to remain who you're called to be even during the times of being worn out. We are who God says we are, we can stand sure of it.

For those of you looking at yourself as worthless, broken, and worn out God is a restorer. He is doing work on the inside and outside. He is going to make all things new. When He puts the finishing touches on you, all eyes will be on you!

ONE IDEA

I've heard several people and even my mentor say, "YOU'RE ONLY ONE GOOD IDEA AWAY," and so the thing about us is that we look for that one good thing to be at the start when it very well may not be. She would share this with us on our group calls because I BELIEVE she knew that within a few of us, we felt a little discouraged because even though things were being done, it still felt as if nothing was happening. So, she would encourage us to keep going even when let me say, I didn't feel like I wanted to. As this phrase rung in my spirit one day, I caught a moment that MOTIVATED me and helped me to grab hold of what was being said.

When I started reading and studying the Bible, as I read Genesis and how God created everything, I asked and wondered why He waited to create man. He did everything else and because we see it how it is and not how it was, we say we would do it like this or that, not considering the why. Creation was strategically done. There had to have been something to place man in and be over, so He created it. He moved in patience by placing everything where it needed to be. So just BEE "N'COURAGED" knowing that what you are purposed to do may not look to you to be coming together, but know it's strategically being done. So, as you get to that ONE, know that it's increasing your creativity, it's increasing your faith, it's increasing your patience and your humility, and your strength to stand and say, "GOD DID IT. AND IT IS GOOD." It's a process; stay in it.

My Apostle spoke these words that I bring to encourage you: "DON'T GET DISCOURAGED IF THE BEST HASN'T COME YET, IT'S YET TO COME."

So, BEE "N'COURAGED" today to keep going.

PRAYER CONCERNING YOU

I'd like to take this time and leave you with words of encouragement in prayer for you.

1 Samuel 30:6, Now David was greatly distressed for the people spoke of stoning him because the soul of all the people was grieved, every man for himself and his daughters, but David strengthened himself in the Lord his God.

There's a song that says, "On Christ the solid rock I stand, all other ground is sinking sand, all other ground is sinking sand."

My prayer for you is that you are ever increasing in the things of God. My prayer is that you now (if you didn't before) see yourself through the eyes of Jesus. Seek out who you are through the eyes and heart of God. His opinion of you is the only one that makes a difference. My prayer for you is that you run after the One Who already has you. Let your desire be, to know Him better, more intimately. He has shown us in His Word what He requires of us: to do justly, love mercifully, and walk humbly with Him. So, my prayer is that during this time of the process, you are strengthened even the more to sacrifice unto God. Because only what we do for Him will last.

Stay in it, stay focused. I pray this is a blessing to you, that you are "N'COURAGED" and strengthened to walk through your process being "N'COURAGED" not just for you, but also for the need of others. To help them through their process of being "N'COURAGED". So, they, in return, will be able to do the same for someone else.

Contact The Author

skdbiz@hotmail.com

https://www.facebook.com/sheronda.davis.9

https://skdbiz.bigcartel.com

Made in the USA
Columbia, SC
23 September 2019